IMAGES
of America

THE OKLAHOMA
STATE CAPITOL

Since construction of the Oklahoma State Capitol commenced in 1914, the inclusion of an ornamental dome was a source of controversy. The dome was deemed too expensive, and was omitted from the final plans. Over the years, many different proposals came about to crown the building. This rendering from 1992 was proposed by the Capitol DOMERS, an organization formed to raise private funding for the construction of a dome. (Courtesy of the Oklahoma Historical Society.)

ON THE COVER: This undated photograph, likely taken in the late 1940s or early 1950s, shows the capitol surrounded by oil derricks. The derricks would come to define the landscape around the building, even becoming tourist attractions. Today, there are two derricks remaining on the immediate grounds adjacent to the capitol, the most iconic being State Capitol Well No. 1. Both wells are no longer active. (Courtesy of the Oklahoma Historical Society.)

IMAGES
of America

THE OKLAHOMA STATE CAPITOL

Trait Thompson

ARCADIA
PUBLISHING

Copyright © 2022 by Trait Thompson
ISBN 978-1-4671-0827-0

Published by Arcadia Publishing
Charleston, South Carolina

Printed in the United States of America

Library of Congress Control Number: 2022937198

For all general information, please contact Arcadia Publishing:
Telephone 843-853-2070
Fax 843-853-0044
E-mail sales@arcadiapublishing.com
For customer service and orders:
Toll-Free 1-888-313-2665

Visit us on the Internet at www.arcadiapublishing.com

*To my wife, Sara, and my children Cale and Lilah.
Your steadfast support and encouragement mean
more to me than you can ever imagine.*

CONTENTS

ACKNOWLEDGMENTS

I could not have completed this book without the help of the wonderful staff at the Oklahoma Historical Society. Research director Chad Williams was instrumental in helping me locate long-forgotten photographs and select the perfect ones for inclusion in this work. I would also like to acknowledge Katherine Coley, Rachel Mosman, Jon May, Jim Meeks, Preston Ware, and Dayna Robinson for their assistance.

My parents, Donald and Tracey Kiesling and Dwain and Angie Thompson, have always encouraged my love of history, and I am indebted to them for always supporting my educational pursuits and cheering me on in the arena of life.

Nobody has done as much to foster my love of history as my high school history teacher Dr. William L. "Bill" Graves. May he rest in peace.

I started working at the Oklahoma State Capitol in December 2010 as a staffer in the Senate for president pro tempore Brian Bingman. I fell in love with the building, and I will always be grateful to Senator Bingman for appointing me to the Capitol Preservation Commission.

The director of the Oklahoma Office of Management and Enterprise Services, Preston Doerflinger, took a chance on me when he hired me to be the project manager for the capitol restoration project in 2014. The project was one of the most challenging and gratifying things I have ever done in my life. I am grateful he gave me the opportunity to do something I loved.

All photographs in this book were provided by the Oklahoma Historical Society. Any errors contained within these pages are mine alone.

INTRODUCTION

By the time Gov. Lee Cruce swung his silver-plated pickax into the ground on July 20, 1914, to officially start construction on the Oklahoma State Capitol, the citizens had been waiting just under seven years for their government to find its permanent home. Such was the joyous occasion that 5,000 people drove their automobiles, walked, or rode the streetcar to the open spot in the prairie northeast of downtown Oklahoma City. The anticipation in the air was palpable as Governor Cruce set the scene for what was to come by remarking, "Gaze out over this spanning six hundred acres of fertile soil, where the grass and wildflowers flourish and let your patriotic hearts well up within you and rejoice that there are men within the state who can and do accomplish things—big things." Oklahoma City resident Frank L. Murphy was so inspired that he wrote a poem about the new capitol, which included this stanza:

> The walls of marble justice shine.
> The chambers ring with right divine;
> Such building will be strangely grand,
> An ornament to any land.

To say there were monumental expectations for this building was putting it mildly.

The architecture firm of Layton and Smith was selected by the Capitol Building Commission to design the capitol. Solomon Layton had made a name for himself since coming to Oklahoma in 1902. He and his partner, S. Weymuss Smith, were paid 1.5 percent of the total construction cost of $1,515,000 for their work. They hired Jewell Hicks to serve as a draftsman. Their Neoclassical design called for the structure to have an ornamental high dome. In fact, they even consulted an architect in Paris who specialized in domes to validate their design. Unfortunately, it was not to be.

Gov. Robert Williams took office in 1915, and legislation was passed naming him chairman of the Capitol Building Commission. He subsequently affirmed the notion the capitol would not include a dome. With budget estimates for the dome ranging from $180,000 to $500,000, it was not deemed a practical expenditure, given the already limited budget. In 1915, Commissioner W.B. Anthony stated his disagreement with the decision noting, "To erect the building as now planned, without the dome, would be antagonistic to every law of architectural beauty." Governor Williams's opposition was not necessarily against the dome itself, just the cost. In 1916, he remarked, "I am not against putting a dome on the capitol, but I do not think the time is right just now for spending that much money when the state is in need of so many other necessary and useful institutions." Thankfully, the legislature directed that the structural support for a dome be included during construction in case future generations saw fit to add one.

After a competitive bidding process, James Stewart and Company of New York was hired to construct the capitol on July 1, 1915. The company was no stranger to building statehouses, as it had recently completed them for Idaho and Utah. Up to the point of the Stewart Company's takeover, the Capitol Building Commission had overseen the construction of the concrete structure using day labor. The company's contract dictated the building was to be finished by August 1, 1917. Construction proceeded smoothly until granite workers went on strike in March 1916, demanding a pay raise of 50¢ per day. The strike was settled after about 45 days, and the project was soon on schedule again. Despite construction occurring in the still unfinished capitol, the legislature met for the first time in its new home on January 2, 1917.

The capitol was officially completed on June 30, 1917, about a month ahead of schedule. Thanks to the watchful eye of Governor Williams and the superintendent hired by the state, Edward P. Boyd, the project came in on budget. Only one instance of graft was attempted, when two people offered a bribe to Commissioner P.J. Goulding of Enid in 1914 to entice him to select their preferred architect. Goulding referred the matter to the attorney general, and the men were later convicted. Despite the monumental achievement of completing the capitol almost 10 years after statehood, there was no grand celebration. In April, the United States had entered World War I, and the minds of Oklahomans were now focused on a different task at hand.

The development of the grounds around the capitol was significantly delayed due to a lack of funding. In October 1917, a conference was held at Oklahoma A&M to discuss a plan for the grounds; in the meantime, prison labor was brought in to make some improvements. In 1919, renowned landscape architect George Kessler was hired to develop plans for beautifying the grounds. Kessler suggested splitting Lincoln Boulevard, planting trees along the street, and installing sunken gardens. He also recommended the state purchase the land north of the capitol for future development and beautification, a suggestion officials would come to wish they had heeded in subsequent decades. The onset of oil drilling activities on state property around the capitol during the 1930s delayed meaningful landscaping for years.

As early as the mid-1920s, the state government began to outgrow the capitol. The board of affairs began constructing new buildings around the capitol starting with the Oklahoma Historical Society building in 1929. Nevertheless, the state could not keep up with the demand for office space, and monumental corridors, ceremonial rooms, and even the staircases were converted into office space. It was not until the 1990s that preservation of the historic character of the building became important to state officials.

The interior walls of the statehouse remained unadorned until November 11, 1928. The first artwork for the capitol, entitled *Pro Patria*, was officially dedicated that day. Commissioned by Frank Phillips and painted by Gilbert White, the triptych was a tribute to Oklahoma soldiers who died during World War I. The first exterior sculpture installed on the grounds was *Tribute to the Romantic Riders of the Range* by Constance Whitney Warren in 1930. In 1983, the legislature created the Capitol Preservation Commission to ensure museum quality art would be displayed in the building and that art placed in the building would relate to the history of Oklahoma. Thanks to the efforts of people like Betty Price and Sen. Charles Ford, the capitol is now teeming with incredible works of art by artists of various backgrounds and styles.

In 2002, after decades of proposals to formally cap the capitol, including the installation of an office tower, an ornamental dome was finally placed on the building. Seeking to commemorate the statehood centennial, Gov. Frank Keating embarked on the ambitious goal of raising private donations to finance the $21 million venture. Nobody had attempted to put a high dome on an existing building since it was done at the US Capitol in 1863, but the Capitol Dome Builders team was up to the task. After 85 years, the Oklahoma State Capitol was officially complete.

One

REMOVAL FROM GUTHRIE

1889–1913

The railroad station at what would become Guthrie, Oklahoma, was established in March 1887 and originally known as Deer Creek. The station was a stop on the north-south Southern Kansas Railway. The name was selected to honor Kansas judge John Guthrie. On the day of the first land run, hundreds of land-seekers disembarked at this station in hope of staking a claim and making a fresh start.

The town of Guthrie sprung up within hours of the opening of the Unassigned Lands in Indian Territory on April 22, 1889. Because townsites could only be 320 acres, there were originally four townsites within the same geographic area. The towns of Guthrie, West Guthrie, East Guthrie, and Capital Hill coexisted with their own governance structures until they consolidated in mid-1890. The passage of the Organic Act in May 1890 officially recognized Oklahoma as a territory and established Guthrie as the capital. This set up a rivalry with Oklahoma City for the state's center of power that would play out over the next two decades.

By the time the Oklahoma Constitutional Convention convened in November 1906, numerous attempts had been made by the territorial legislature to relocate the capital. The convention delegates attempted to establish a permanent capital but were also unsuccessful. The Enabling Act of 1906 established the capital at Guthrie until 1913, but that provision was struck down by the US Supreme Court in 1911 as unconstitutional.

Guthrie City Hall was designed by Joseph Foucart and constructed at a cost of $25,000 in 1902. The second floor of the building featured an assembly room that was used for civic meetings and ceremonial events. Use of the room was denied to Carrie Nation in 1906 for one of her prohibition events. Most famously, the assembly room served as the site of the Oklahoma Constitutional Convention from 1906 to 1907. The building was demolished in 1955.

The campaign for ratification of the Oklahoma Constitution by the people of Oklahoma was fierce at times. The Republicans were against approval and Vice Pres. William Howard Taft complained that it was a set of bylaws instead of a constitution. William Jennings Bryan barnstormed the state advocating for its passage. Kate Barnard characterized the document as being "more of human liberty than anything written since the Declaration of Independence."

On September 17, 1907, the Oklahoma Constitution was put to a vote of the people for ratification. Ratification was almost a foregone conclusion as Republicans had the unenviable task of campaigning against the document that would finally grant statehood to Oklahoma Territory. After the votes were tallied, 71 percent of voters registered their approval of the constitution.

Despite territorial governor Frank Frantz's appeal to Theodore Roosevelt to reject the constitution, the president indicated his intent to sign the statehood proclamation on November 16, 1907. That morning, at 9:16 a.m. Central Time, he did just that. Over 30,000 people were in Guthrie to witness the historic occasion of Oklahoma's entry into the Union as the 46th state. Spectators gathered for over three hours in front of Carnegie Library to hear speeches from Oklahoma's new elected officials. To symbolize the union of Indian Territory and Oklahoma Territory into one state, a mock wedding was held between Anna Bennett of Muskogee and Charles Jones of Oklahoma City. When the ceremonies concluded, visitors to Guthrie were treated to a grand parade and a free barbecue.

Charles N. Haskell was born in Ohio in 1850. After receiving his teaching certificate, he became an attorney in 1880 and moved to Muskogee by 1901. He became active in city politics and was elected to serve as a delegate to the Sequoyah Constitutional Convention in 1905, where he was chosen to be vice president. The Sequoyah Convention served as a warm-up act for his work at the Oklahoma Constitutional Convention in 1906. In tandem with William "Alfalfa Bill" Murray, Haskell was able to steer the direction of the convention and bring it to its successful conclusion. After being inaugurated as Oklahoma's first governor in 1907, he began to grow weary of the political attacks that came from Guthrie, a Republican town. Haskell worked to get an initiative petition on the ballot to move the capital. After getting the required number of signatures, he set the election date for Saturday, June 11, 1910. Oklahomans would choose between Guthrie, Oklahoma City, and Shawnee.

These photographs show the Logan County Courthouse and the governor's office inside the courthouse. The courthouse was constructed in 1907 by Manhattan Construction, and in addition to serving as the headquarters for Logan County's offices, it was the state capitol. County leaders leased office space in the courthouse to the state for $1 per year. The courthouse was the site of one of the most controversial aspects of the 1910 capital election when Governor Haskell's aide W.B. Anthony drove to Guthrie from Oklahoma City the night the polls closed and smuggled the official state seal out of the building in a bundle of laundry.

THE HEART OF OKLAHOMA CITY FROM LITTLE FRANKS BALLOON *COPYRIGHT 1910 BY FA STERN*

By 1910, Oklahoma City was a growing city with a population of over 64,000—almost double the number living there at statehood. By comparison, Guthrie had a little over 11,000 residents. Oklahoma City had become the business and commercial hub of the state. Construction of new buildings was so rapid that six brick and tile companies were in operation to keep up with demand.

The citizens of Guthrie, seeking to gain a foothold on the capital, authorized a bond issue in the amount of $150,000 in 1905 to build Convention Hall. The building was to serve as the legislature's permanent home. It was finished in 1909 in time for the legislature to meet there that year. The legislature would only meet there one more time before moving to Oklahoma City.

This photograph, taken in 1979, shows the interior of Convention Hall in Guthrie. In the run-up to the second statewide election to determine Oklahoma's capital in 1912, the *Daily Oklahoman* published an article criticizing the amount of rent the state paid when the capital was in Guthrie and remarked, "Convention Hall has been tried and found wanting." In 1919, the property was sold to the Scottish Rite Masons.

This rather verbose roadside billboard touted the advantages of moving the capital to Oklahoma City in advance of the June 11, 1910, election. In addition to showcasing the city's prominent buildings (many of which would be demolished during Urban Renewal), it reads, "The Capital should be in the city of greatest achievement." It also notes the promise of building a free capitol using proceeds from land sales near the new building.

This postcard was circulated to entice people to vote for Oklahoma City as the new capital. In May 1910, Oklahoma City business leaders wrote a letter to Governor Haskell stating, "It must be apparent that Oklahoma City has a larger interest in a speedy, economical and safe location of the state's permanent capital than any other single community in the state." The building used in the photograph is the Kansas Statehouse.

As expected, Oklahoma City carried the day in the election to select a new capital for the 46th state. However, citizens of Guthrie immediately brought lawsuits in the state supreme court and in federal court. In November 1910, the state supreme court invalidated the results of the election due to improper ballot language. The capital fight was not over yet.

LEE-HUCKINS HOTEL. OKLAHOMA CITY, OKLAHOMA. JUNE 12, 1910.

Governor Haskell received the results of the capital relocation election while he was in Tulsa. When he arrived in Oklahoma City, he established the new capitol at the Lee-Huckins Hotel. This photograph, dated June 12, 1910, commemorates his first official act in the new capital—the signing of diplomas for the graduating class of the University of Oklahoma.

Real estate developer Israel M. Putnam and his partners donated 1,600 acres of land northwest of Oklahoma City for the new capitol. Lots near the location of the new building would be sold to finance the construction of the edifice. Despite the governor's support for the location, it was ultimately nixed by the Senate due to its distance from downtown Oklahoma City and its proximity to a packing plant.

19

The Irving School was constructed in 1896 at NE Fourth Street and Walnut Avenue and served as the first permanent high school building for Oklahoma City. In August 1910, Governor Haskell and several state agencies, including the secretary of state, moved into the school. The school served as the capitol until 1917 and was destroyed by fire in 1937.

On November 28, 1910, a special session of the legislature convened in the Levy Building in Oklahoma City to decide the location of the new state capital. They chose Oklahoma City and elected to locate the new capitol on land donated by William Harn and John Culbertson two miles northeast of downtown. It would take another statewide election on November 5, 1912, before the matter was settled for good.

Two

Construction of the Capitol

1914–1917

As Gov. Lee Cruce made his way to the ground-breaking ceremony for the new state capitol on July 20, 1914, he may have reflected on the difficulties that were overcome to get to this momentous day. In the 1913 legislative session, $750,000 was appropriated to start work contingent on Oklahoma City paying the state $53,573.50. After further litigation in the courts throughout 1913, the long-awaited capitol was about to become a reality.

Gov Cruce Turning First Dirt
For State Capitol Building
Oklahoma City July 20 1914.

At 10:30 a.m. on July 20, 1914, Gov. Lee Cruce sunk his silver-plated pickax into the soil and officially commenced work on the Oklahoma State Capitol. A crowd of over 5,000 spectators braved the hot weather to witness the event. Dust hung in the air like a cloud as movie cameras from the Universal Film Company recorded the festivities to be played in theaters all over the country. The ceremony was not without its surprises, however. Anna Laskey, previously denied an opportunity to participate, stepped in front of the governor and began throwing dirt. Later, in his remarks, Governor Cruce said, "This is not a time for speechmaking, but a time for work. Talking may be all right in arranging and planning for a state capitol, but talking never built a state capitol and never will. It takes work, good, hard, honest labor to build such an edifice as we are starting today."

The legislature authorized the capitol to be three stories tall. Yet the building needed to be large enough to accommodate all state government offices to avoid paying unnecessary rent. To work around this problem, the building's planners designated a sub-basement, basement, mezzanine, and attic. Today, this is the second floor of the building, but when the capitol opened, it was the first floor.

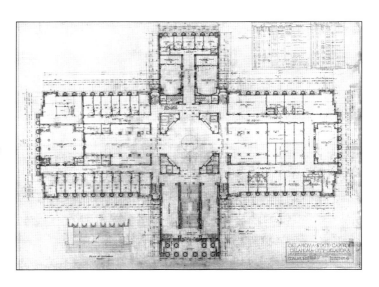

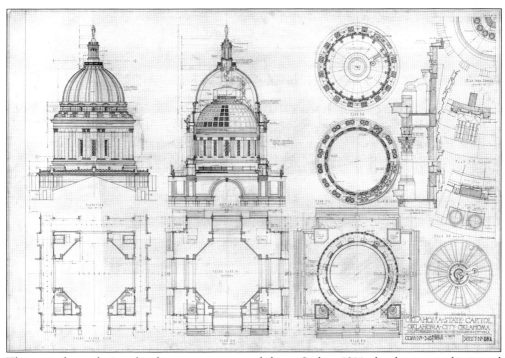

The capitol was designed to have an ornamental dome. In late 1914, the dome was eliminated from construction plans due to its cost. Governor Williams favored spending the estimated $250,000 the dome would have cost to establish a state hospital instead. The legislature and Capitol Building Commission had the foresight to include the footings and structural support necessary to add a dome in the future.

By the time Solomon Layton's firm, Layton and Smith, won the bid to design the capitol, he was already one of the most prominent architects in the state. Layton came to Oklahoma in 1902, and throughout his illustrious career, designed over 100 commercial, educational, and public buildings. In a 1917 *Daily Oklahoman* article, the contractors credited the architects for the capitol's "beauty of design" and "accuracy of specifications."

Before he became Oklahoma's third governor in 1915, Robert Williams had been an attorney, delegate to the Oklahoma Constitutional Convention, and chief justice of the state supreme court. Legislation passed in 1915 put him in charge of the State Capitol Commission, and he oversaw every detail of the building's construction over the next two years. He even moved into the building early so he could watch over the contractors.

This photograph, dated April 19, 1915, shows the reinforced concrete structure of the capitol under construction. Steel rebar and lumber rest in the foreground, ready to be used in the formation of the building's concrete pillars and beams. Prior to a contractor being hired, the Capitol Building Commission hired day laborers to complete the structure up to the mezzanine level. It was estimated the commission's initiative saved the state $25,000.

By June 1915, the structure was complete on the first floor (today's second floor). Modern observers might note the lack of a circular opening in the center of the rotunda. After attorney general S.P. Freeling objected to his office being in the basement (today's first floor), the structure was modified with an opening on the floor above to satisfy him.

The day labor crew hired to construct the structure of the capitol pauses for a photograph on April 28, 1915. The capitol was built during the Progressive Era in American history, and labor issues were at the forefront during construction. A 1913 editorial in the *Oklahoma Labor Unit* pushed back on the suggestion by some legislators that convict labor should be used in erecting

Apr. 28th. 1915.

Photo. By. Garland B. Hale.

the capitol. A 1915 article in the *Daily Ardmoreite* noted that "a strict union wage" was being paid to the workers. In March 1916, granite cutters went on strike demanding a 50¢-per-day increase. The strike spread to the other trades before labor and management reached an agreement a month later. Despite the setback, the project remained on schedule.

According to a May 28, 1915, article in the *Daily Admoreite* newspaper, a million feet of lumber had been used up to that point for the forms used in pouring the concrete. Over 15 tons of steel were used in the concrete footings of the structural columns. The paper also declared that no other capitol "will equal it in the thoroughness of its modern arrangement."

Many capitols from other states were built in or near a city's downtown area, close to the commercial hub of activity. As this photograph of John Long illustrates, the Oklahoma Capitol was constructed in the midst of prime farmland, about two miles from downtown Oklahoma City. The promise of free land compelled legislators to overlook any inconveniences due to the location.

On July 1, 1915, the Capitol Building Commission selected James Stewart and Company from New York as the general contractor to complete the construction of the Oklahoma Capitol. Its bid of $1,253,500 was the lowest of the submissions, which included three Oklahoma companies. James Stewart and Company had previously constructed the Utah and Idaho Capitols, and would later build the Scottish Rite Masonic Temple in Guthrie.

The Capitol Building Commission hired Edward P. Boyd to supervise the construction of the capitol on behalf of the state. An engineer for the federal government, Boyd came to Oklahoma City in 1910 to build the post office. Governor Cruce convinced Pres. Woodrow Wilson to loan Boyd to the project. In 1923, he was named the dean of the engineering department at Oklahoma A&M.

Oklahoma's capital and capitol were yesterday the cynosure of Oklahoma observation, around which centered the state's proud patriotism

43,370 Week Day Average for October

THE DAILY OKLAHOMAN

48,184 Sunday Average for October

VOL. 27. NO. 52.   OKLAHOMA CITY, OKLAHOMA, WEDNESDAY, NOVEMBER 17, 1915—FOURTEEN PAGES   PRICE FIVE CENTS

REVISION OF LAWS TO COVER FOREIGN CRIMES PROPOSED

10,000 SEE MASONS LAY CAPITOL CORNER STONE WITH INSPIRING CEREMONIES OF ANCIENT LODGE

THE WEATHER

ALLIES MAY URGE GREECE TO DEFINE MILITARY POLICY

VIEWS OF IMPOSING PAGEANT AND SOLEMN RITUAL OF STATEHOOD DAY

Cabinet Will Ask Congress to Change Sherman Anti-Trust Statute.

CONVICTIONS HARD UNDER PRESENT ACT

Enlargement of Secret Service Powers Also May Be Sought.

Safety of Troops in Event of Retreat Matter of Grave Concern.

DIPLOMATS IN EAST MAY OBTAIN DESIRES

Serbians and French Holding Positions, but Pressure Increasing.

STATE VICTOR IN HIGHWAY CONTEST

Jefferson Road Will Pass Through Oklahoma Instead of Arkansas.

OFFICERS SELECTED

Louisiana, Texas, Missouri, Iowa and Minnesota Also on the Route.

The cornerstone for the state capitol was laid on November 16, 1915. Newspapers estimated between 10,000 and 15,0000 people were present to watch the four-ton block of Tishomingo granite be placed into its permanent location. The cornerstone ceremony was presided over by the Masons. In the photograph below, grand master Almer Monroney consecrates the cornerstone as his 13-year-old son A.S. "Mike" Monroney looks on. Fifty items were placed in the cornerstone, including copies of newspapers, a Bible, and a copy of the Oklahoma Constitution. After the ceremony, the *Daily Oklahoman* wrote, "Yesterday it was a chunk of stone—that and nothing more; today it is a sacred thing, a living thing, almost an immortal thing to the hundreds and hundreds of thousands that live and labor and love and—sometimes—suffer in this fair commonwealth."

By the end of 1915, the concrete skeleton for the capitol was nearing completion. In this view of the southeast side of the building, the railroad spur to the job site is evident in the foreground with several boxcars on the track. Soon after the ground-breaking ceremony in 1914, the Capitol Building Commission determined the spur was necessary to get building materials to the grounds as quickly as possible.

Today, Lincoln Boulevard is an expressway with three lanes of traffic moving at rapid speeds in both directions. That was not the case in early 1916, as evidenced by these men approaching the south side of the building on a one-lane Lincoln Boulevard, recently muddied by spring rains.

This view looking northeast shows the Senate chamber under construction in May 1916. Hollow tile blocks purchased by the Humboldt Brick Manufacturing Company make up the interior wall structures, which would later be covered in plaster. Skylights were originally installed to provide natural lighting to the decorative stained-glass insets in the ornamental plaster ceiling. Metal air ducts in the walls provided a system of distributing fresh air throughout the building.

Despite its prevalence today, concrete as a structural building material was relatively new when this photograph was taken in 1916. At the time, it was believed the capitol was the largest reinforced concrete building in the world. To ensure it could bear the expected load, tests were arranged. The sign attached to the hollow tile blocks reads, "500000 lbs test load concrete girder 54 ft span."

By the summer of 1916, the concrete structure of the capitol was finished, and the installation of the limestone cladding on the building's exterior was well underway. The delays caused by the labor strike in spring 1916 had been overcome and it was noted in the July 30, 1916, edition of the *Daily Oklahoman* that the project was four to six months ahead of schedule.

Streetcars were a primary mode of transportation in 1916 when this photograph was taken. At one time, Oklahoma City had three streetcar companies competing for business. The line going to the capitol was operated by the Oklahoma City Land and Development Company (owned by William Harn), but it was colloquially known as the Yellow Mule Line because there was only one yellow car, and it "bucked like a mule."

While some legislators desired only native Oklahoma stone to be used in the capitol, a bill passed in 1915 directed the Capitol Building Commission to seek out the "best quality." The decision was made to use pink granite for the sub-basement and basement levels from a quarry known as Ten Acre Rock near Troy, Oklahoma. A total of 34,000 cubic feet of granite was transported to Oklahoma City and cut and finished on the job site by 100 stonemasons. Hoosier Silver Gray Indiana limestone was used for the remaining levels. The limestone was finished in Bedford, Indiana, and the ornamental carving was overseen by Crescenzo Di Donato, a native of Italy. Each of the Corinthian capitals on the building comprised 250 cubic feet of limestone, and in total, over 161,000 cubic feet of stone was shipped to Oklahoma City in train cars.

FIRST JOINT SESSION OKLAHOMA STATE LEGISLATURE
NEW CAPITAL BUILDING JAN. 19, 1917.

PHOTO BY
THAT MAN STONE
OKLAHOMA CITY

The terms of the contract signed by James Stewart and Company stipulated both legislative chambers and committee rooms be ready for occupation by January 1, 1917. The entirety of the capitol construction project was to be complete by August 1, 1917. As the date drew closer for the legislature to convene in session, some legislators began to express doubt the building would be ready. It was suggested the legislature should convene on January 2, 1917, and immediately adjourn until the summer. Governor Williams was against that proposal due to the projected cost of $5,000 to rent space in a downtown office building for another session. The legislature did gavel into session as scheduled, but some of the committee rooms remained unfinished. There was also no telephone service or drinking water in the capitol. Rep. D.B. Collums would later reminisce, "When the pounding of the hammers got too loud, the legislature had to adjourn for the day, or else go into some other part of the building."

By the time this photograph was taken on March 2, 1917, the legislature was meeting in the capitol, and Governor Williams had moved into the building so he could monitor the last few months of work. In one instance, Williams became irate over a slightly discolored block of limestone on the south side of the building and demanded it be removed. After arbitration, the stone was left in place.

Almost 10 years after statehood, the capitol was completed on June 30, 1917. The January 7, 1917, edition of the *Daily Oklahoman* reported, "There is no building in the state that begins to approach the statehouse in size, cost or beauty. Oklahoma's capitol building ranks favorably among similar institutions in the United States and is superior to a number of structures boasted of by states much older than Oklahoma."

The second-floor (today's fourth floor) rotunda in the finished building was a masterpiece of ornamental architecture. The Alabama marble floors and the marble balustrade project a pristine image combined with the soaring ceiling height and exquisite plaster column capitals. Due to budget limitations, the walls in this area were only painted with a dark wainscot, and sculptures were not installed in the niches.

Flanking both sides of the grand staircase on the second floor (today's fourth floor), were two identical monumental corridors with marble floors, high ceilings, and decorative light fixtures. The south wall of both corridors was later adorned with panels of the *Pro Patria* painting. In 1976, these corridors were converted into legislative committee rooms.

Located on the first floor (today's second floor) in the west wing, the supreme court showcased a lavish plaster ceiling and four large columns made of Vermont marble topped with plaster capitals. The mahogany bench and bar were both hand-carved. Quotes from Justinian and Cicero were carved into marble plaques near the ceiling on the north and south walls, respectively.

A January 7, 1917, article in the *Daily Oklahoman* characterized the grand stairway as one of the most "beautiful and impressive" areas in the capitol. The article also noted the visitor has a clear view from the base of the stairway into the low dome, a distance of 170 feet. The semi-circular ceiling above is adorned with stained-glass skylights, 75 feet above the first floor.

Three

GROWING INTO THE CAPITOL

1918–1930

The awe-inspiring second-floor rotunda (today's fourth floor) of the newly completed capitol was an architectural marvel. However, that did not stop some people from abusing the new seat of state government. After two men were arrested for kicking over a cuspidor during a bout of horseplay in 1917, capitol officials expressed frustration that visitors had been routinely disfiguring the walls and spitting upon the floors.

This early photograph of the Senate chamber was taken shortly after construction was complete. The Senate chamber is in the east wing of the capitol and is two stories high. The chamber had an abundance of natural light due to the skylights and clerestory windows. Wall lamps on the chamber floor and sconces in the gallery provided additional illumination.

The two-story corridor adjacent to the east side of the grand staircase was used as a display area for the Oklahoma Historical Society. Other monumental corridors in the building also began to be used for necessary functions as the state outgrew the allotted office space in the capitol. By 1919, state officials were discussing whether they should add on to the capitol or construct other buildings.

In 1919, legislation was passed authorizing the state to hire George E. Kessler, renowned landscape architect and civic planner from St. Louis, to design the exterior environment around the capitol. Kessler's vision called for a grand approach on Lincoln Boulevard from the south, which would split at Sixteenth Street allowing for unobstructed views of the building. Kessler designed an open sunken garden and lawn directly south of the building and four rows of trees on each side of the boulevard. Provisions were also made for two state buildings to be constructed south of the capitol, two to the north, and one each on the east and west sides. To realize the plan, the seventh legislature provided $200,000 to purchase 35 acres of land south of the capitol and 19 acres north of it. Land was also to be acquired to the east and west of Lincoln Boulevard, some of it owned by the original capitol benefactors William Harn and John Culbertson. Kessler was paid $5,000 by the state for his work.

In this photograph, members of the Oklahoma National Guard present the colors on the front steps of the capitol in 1919. In previous years, the Oklahoma National Guard had served on the Mexican border in 1916 and 1917 and later deployed to France as part of the 142nd Regiment of the 36th Infantry Division. After the war ended, they returned home and were discharged in July 1919.

The focal point in this busy scene in the capitol's second-floor rotunda (today's fourth floor) is a large-scale model of a memorial arch to commemorate the service of Oklahomans in World War I. As part of George Kessler's grounds design, the arch was to be designed by Layton, Smith & Forsyth and placed where Lincoln Boulevard split at NE Sixteenth Street. It would be 50 feet tall and 150 feet wide.

The condition of the southwest grounds around the capitol in 1920 illustrated the need for George Kessler's improvement plan. According to a July 27, 1922, article in the *Duncan Weekly Eagle*, the capitol was "surrounded by tall weeds, junk heaps and other scenery classed as 'cornfields.'"

Offices in the capitol were equipped with all the modern conveniences available in 1920. This photograph of Judge Stewart and Lucille Snider shows a telephone, electric fan, and a light switch on the wall. Additionally, the building featured an internal vacuum system, an automatic heat-regulating system, and an ice plant for cooling the air in the summer.

Located directly across the street from the capitol at 523 NE Twenty-Third Street was the Hazer Feed Store, a fixture in that location for many years. Later owner Samuel Hazer renamed it the Capitol Feed Store. Hazer was an immigrant from Syria who came to Oklahoma by way of Illinois.

By 1922, scant progress had been made on George Kessler's landscaping plan. Lincoln Boulevard had not yet been developed into the "V" pattern that would provide a grand approach from the south and the road was little more than a dirt path to the statehouse. In many ways, the exterior environment had a long way to go before it matched the stately nature of the capitol.

John "Jack" Calloway Walton was a rising star in Oklahoma politics when he was elected governor in 1922. He had previously served as mayor of Oklahoma City and during that time gained a reputation as being a friend of farmers and laborers. Instead of hosting an inaugural ball after he was elected governor, he held a massive barbecue at the Oklahoma City fairgrounds attended by over 100,000 citizens. His popularity was to be short-lived. The governor alienated the legislature with harsh tactics to get legislation passed and removed members of the Board of Regents for the state's major universities in favor of his friends. His downfall came when he decided to vigorously oppose the Ku Klux Klan in hopes of boosting his national political prospects. After declaring statewide martial law to curb the Klan, legislators, several of whom were Klan members, had enough and attempted to convene at the capitol in September 1923 to impeach him. Walton activated the National Guard and blocked the legislators from accessing the House and Senate chambers. By November, Walton was impeached and out of office.

In this photograph taken in 1926, the Oklahoma City Fire Department shows off its equipment and personnel. The department began as a volunteer force in 1894 with a donated horse-drawn wagon and resided in one building. The first motorized vehicle was purchased in 1910. By 1919, the two-platoon system was implemented, with A and B shifts for personnel.

Famed aviator Charles Lindbergh, who had completed the first solo trans-Atlantic flight in May 1927, visited Oklahoma City on September 28, 1927. Lindbergh flew his famous plane, the *Spirit of St. Louis*, to Municipal Airport that afternoon and was subsequently greeted by thousands of spectators before climbing into a car with Gov. Henry Johnston for a long parade through Oklahoma City. This image shows Lindbergh approaching the capitol on Lincoln Boulevard.

The turbulence in Oklahoma politics during the 1920s continued when Governor Johnston activated the National Guard in December 1927 to prevent the legislature from investigating his conduct. The governor deemed the legislative assembly an illegal action. Dubbed the "Ewe Lamb Rebellion," the legislature's attempt to impeach the governor over petty matters fizzled out as the Christmas holidays approached.

The legislature's ire with Governor Johnston began boiling again when he supported Al Smith's bid for the presidency. Smith's Catholic faith and views opposing prohibition were at odds with many in Oklahoma. In this photograph, Governor Johnston is seen on the left side of the table (third from the front) during his impeachment trial in January 1929, in the Senate chamber. He was later impeached on the charge of incompetency.

In 1927, the legislature appropriated $75,000 to build the second building in the capitol complex: the governor's mansion. The architecture firm of Layton, Hicks, and Forsyth designed the mansion to have a limestone façade and be compatible with the capitol's design. The mansion was completed in October 1928. Governor Johnston and his family lived there for only a few months before he was impeached.

This photograph shows the Oklahoma Governor's Mansion in 1928 from the east steps of the capitol. Concerned that the small structure would not look right near the capitol, it was located on a five-acre tract of land a short distance away. The front of the mansion was designed to face the statehouse. The meager budget for construction left no money for landscaping the grounds.

In February 1929, the legislature authorized $500,000 to construct the third building in the capitol complex, designated for the Oklahoma Historical Society. The building was designed by Layton, Hicks, and Forsyth and was modeled after the Minnesota Historical Society building. It was also to serve as a war memorial with dedicated meeting space and offices for veteran groups. Construction was completed in 1930.

The under-construction Oklahoma Historical Society building at far right gives a clue about when this undated photograph was taken. On January 9, 1930, a massive cold spell and snowstorm engulfed central Oklahoma with over 12 inches of snow falling overnight. An article in the January 10, 1930, *Daily Oklahoman* called it the "worst snow blanket experienced in years."

This view looking north on Lincoln Boulevard to the capitol shows some progress had been made by the late 1920s on George Kessler's landscaping plan. There was no sunken garden or trees planted, but sod had been installed with a sprinkler system. An August 3, 1928, article in the *Daily Oklahoman* noted six floodlights had been installed to illuminate the capitol's front façade.

Since the capitol was built, it has served as a great backdrop for all manner of photographs. In this undated image, young ladies pose on a stylish 1930 Packard 740 Series automobile. The vehicle sold for $3,200 in 1930, which is approximately $52,000 in today's dollars.

Constance Whitney Warren sculpted *Tribute to the Romantic Riders of the Range* and the piece was arranged to be donated to the state by her father, George Henry Warren. Despite the wording on the plaque, the statue was not dedicated by Will Rogers in 1930. Rogers was unable to attend the scheduled ceremony, and it was not formally dedicated until 1957. A sister statue resides on the grounds of the Texas Capitol.

This aerial photograph of the state capitol and grounds was most likely taken in 1930. The Oklahoma Historical Society building is seen under construction on the lower right and the new statue by Constance Whitney Warren has yet to be placed on the plaza south of the main entrance.

The end of the 1920s marked the beginning of an urban oil boom with the discovery of the Oklahoma City Field. Oklahoma City Well No. 1 was completed on December 4, 1928, south of the city limits, and by 1930, wells were being drilled inside the city. By the mid-1930s, George Kessler's vision for the capitol grounds was dealt a death blow as state leaders acquiesced to drilling around the building.

The view is to the east on NE Twenty-Third Street in this photograph taken in late 1930. In 1929, William F. Harn, unhappy with how the state had maintained its land around the capitol, decided to lease out 100 acres of his adjacent land for oil drilling. He explained, "I fail to see how erection of an oil derrick could make property adjoining the capitol any more unsightly than it now is."

Four

OIL COMES TO
THE CAPITOL

1931–1950

Thousands of dancers crowded into the capitol to celebrate the inauguration of Gov. William H. "Alfalfa Bill" Murray on the evening of January 12, 1931. According to the next day's *Daily Oklahoman*, National Guard soldiers had to clear a spot for the new governor to dance with his wife at the ball. He took his leave from the raucous gathering around 11:00 p.m. to retire to his hotel.

At the time this photograph was taken in late 1931, Guy Roush had served as a taxidermist for the State of Oklahoma for 12 years. His work studio was in the hidden recesses of the capitol's attic. An employee of the Game and Fish Commission, Roush was paid $100 per month, according to a 1932 article in the *Daily Oklahoman*.

This first-floor corridor in the capitol speaks to the crowded conditions that were beginning to develop in the building by the early 1930s. The corridor is being used as a display area for Roush's taxidermy along with some items in cases. Framed pictures and other materials appear to be stored against the left wall.

Famed aviator Wiley Post poses with his 1932 Ford V8 Coupe at NE Eighteenth Street and Lincoln Boulevard with the capitol in the background. Post was born to a cotton-farming family in Texas in 1898. Seeing his first airplane in 1913 at a fair in Lawton, Oklahoma, he became inspired and enrolled in an aviation school in Kansas City. After World War I, he worked in the Oklahoma oil fields where an accident robbed him of his left eye. He purchased his first plane with money obtained from the settlement. After selling the plane, Post was hired by oilman F.C. Hall to be his private pilot. In 1928, Hall purchased a Lockheed Vega airplane that would become synonymous with Wiley Post, the *Winnie Mae*. In 1930, Post won an air race between Los Angeles and Chicago. Along with his navigator, he circumnavigated the globe in just under nine days in 1931, the first to accomplish such a feat. Post became the first person to fly solo around the world in 1933.

The House of Representatives chamber was illuminated by rays of light streaming through the clerestory windows as Governor Murray gave his annual address to a joint session of the legislature on January 3, 1933. During his address, the governor petitioned the lawmakers to divert a portion of the gasoline tax to help pay down the state's deficit and to pass a state income tax.

Charles N. Haskell was elected the state's first governor in 1907. He was responsible for the relocation of the capital city from Guthrie to Oklahoma City in 1910. After his death in July 1933, he laid in state in the Blue Room where thousands of citizens came to pay their respects. Haskell's close friend, Governor Murray, lingered near the bier for over an hour.

This photograph looks north on Lincoln Boulevard from the capitol grounds. Over the years, state officials had expressed their desires to purchase the property surrounding the capitol north of NE Twenty-Third Street, yet it had not occurred by the time this photograph was taken in August 1934. A 1936 report by the planning board again suggested that land be acquired north of the building to improve the approach and eliminate "traffic difficulties."

The federal government created the Civil Works Administration (CWA) to provide temporary construction work for Americans during the harsh winter of 1933–1934 when this photograph was taken. The board of affairs used the program to hire Oklahomans for remodeling and repainting work in the capitol during the spring of 1934. The project was temporarily halted when the CWA was terminated in March 1934, but it resumed later that summer.

The atmosphere in the House of Representatives was tense on February 21, 1935, as members debated whether relief funds should be distributed by county commissioners rather than a federal relief committee. After Rep. H.O. Boggs and Rep. L.D. Armstrong exchanged heated words, Boggs charged with arms swinging but was blocked by other members. He subsequently jumped on a desk and voiced his protest.

Donald Gordon, parks superintendent for Oklahoma City, prepared a plan for extensive landscaping improvements on the capitol grounds that was approved by the state board of affairs in July 1935. Along with these improvements, funds were made available by the highway commission to pave the cross-sections of Lincoln Boulevard from the capitol south to NE Fourteenth Street.

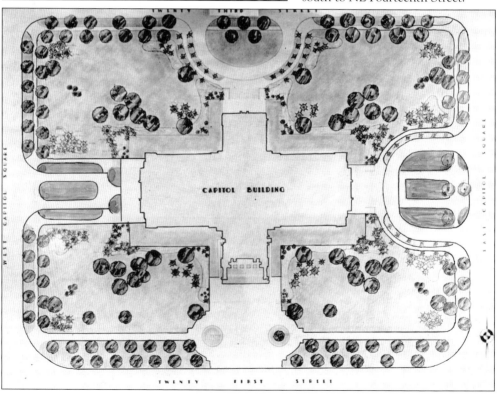

Beloved Oklahoma aviator Wiley Post perished in a plane crash along with his friend, Will Rogers, on August 15, 1935, in Point Barrow, Alaska. On the morning of August 22, Post's body lay in honor in a bronze casket at the capitol, the first person to be given such an honor. Twenty thousand mourners came to the capitol to pay homage to their hero. Doors and windows had to be opened in the building to provide some relief from the stifling August heat exacerbated by the crowd, but even that did not prevent people from fainting. Just after 11:00 a.m., the National Guard closed the doors to the building, keeping an estimated 10,000 people from getting inside. All the while, a dozen private planes circled over the building dropping streamers and flowers in tribute.

This photograph, taken in 1935, shows one of the last views of the capitol grounds and the surrounding area before the Oklahoma City Oilfield was extended to state property. In the coming years, oil derricks would be erected on state property, in some cases just yards from the statehouse.

This tapestry depicting the migration of emigrants in the United States was entitled *Westward the Course of the Empire Takes its Way.* Governor E.W. Marland hung the intricate piece in the Blue Room during his term. The left border of the tapestry contained the portrait of William Clarke and the right border the portrait of Daniel Boone. It took three weavers a total of 23 months to complete.

Since the omission of the dome from the capitol during construction, the issue of providing a proper cap for the building had not abated. Occasionally, a member of the legislature would introduce a bill to add a dome, but the idea never gained traction. Starting in the mid-1920s, as available space in the building began to dwindle, the board of affairs flirted with the idea of adding an office tower instead of a dome. In 1926, the *Tulsa Tribune* responded to the proposal by writing, "Some of the funniest men in Oklahoma are on the State Board of Affairs." The idea fizzled out in the 1920s, but it was resurrected again in 1935 and this rendering was produced to show what an office tower would look like on the building. Board of affairs chairman L.M. Nichols indicated there was $400,000 in the building fund and said the decision to construct the capitol tower would be delayed until the legislature determined whether a new building for the judiciary should be constructed instead.

By early 1936, the Oklahoma City Oil Field had grown around the capitol, but there were no wells on state property due to city zoning ordinances. Frustrated that the state was denied the lucrative revenue source, Gov. E.W. Marland, former owner of the Marland Oil Company, declared martial law, and called out the National Guard to ensure drilling could commence. The courts later ruled that city ordinances did not apply to state property.

The state capitol was located in the prolific Simpson "Wilcox Sand" oil play. The caption on this photograph, dated June 4, 1936, noted, "Wilcox sand is the big pay-off around Oklahoma City." Oil production was known to exceed 20,000 barrels per day during its heyday.

This photograph, looking northwest, captures a unique view of the capitol on September 1, 1936, from the viewpoint of the Lincoln Terrace neighborhood. According to the neighborhood's website, the first homes were built in 1918, and by the end of the 1920s, there were 70 houses, with most of them two stories in the American Colonial, Tudor, or Italian Revival architectural style. The neighborhood continued to develop into the 1930s.

On November 24, 1936, Governor Marland (standing at the microphone) made a speech to open the special session of the 16th legislature. Governor Marland listed 12 priorities, which included providing relief for the unemployed and those affected by the drought. He also discussed the addition of another building in the capitol complex. Speaker J.T. Daniel (right) and Lt. Gov. James Berry (left) are seated behind the governor.

By the end of 1936, the state had signed off on leasing the capitol grounds for oil production in the Lincoln Boulevard median from NE Fifteenth to NE Nineteenth Streets. The tract directly south of the capitol was leased by Sunray Oil Company and Inland Development Company. In this undated photograph, a group of workmen and a team of mules are excavating for the foundation of a new well.

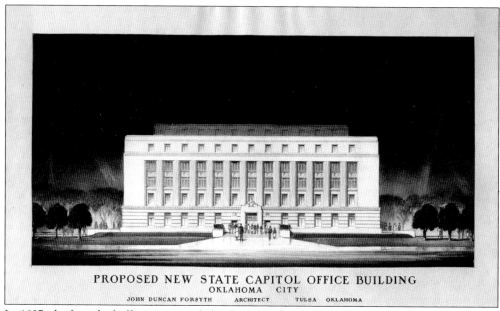

In 1937, the board of affairs approved the design for a new state office building to be located southwest of the capitol, directly across from the historical society building. Tulsa architect John Forsyth was selected to design the new office structure, which would house the public welfare board, highway commission, corporation commission, and tax commission. Oil revenues were earmarked to cover the cost of construction.

Responding to increasing numbers of vehicle accidents and rising crime, the legislature created the Oklahoma Highway Patrol in April 1937. The procession of vehicles in this photograph is part of the first academy graduation on July 1, 1937. During their first year of service, the troopers wrote over 280,000 warnings to Oklahoma drivers who were not accustomed to being monitored on the roads.

Approximately 10,000 people reportedly came out to see Leon Phillips inaugurated as Oklahoma's 11th governor on January 9, 1939. In his speech, Phillips pledged to discharge any state employee who was intoxicated on the job and reaffirmed his support of organized labor. Reporter Otis Sullivant wrote he "read his speech, but put enough fire into it to hold the crowd's attention."

The oil fields around the capitol were typically a hive of activity as workers pumped the valuable commodity. This 1941 photograph shows a group of roughnecks working to recondition one of the wells north of the building. The *Daily Oklahoman* caption indicated 20–30 wells were going through this process.

In the original architectural plans for the capitol, a large open room was planned on the second floor (originally first floor) east wing for agricultural exhibits. The room was later reconfigured as a ladies' lounge and decorated with ornate furniture. This 1940s image shows a mural on the east wall of the room depicting the governor's mansion. Today, this is the governor's large conference room.

State Capitol Well No. 1 was completed by Phillips Petroleum, Sunray Oil Company, and British-American Oil Producing Company in 1942. Each company paid the state $5,000 for the right to drill. Nicknamed "Petunia No. 1" because the well was drilled in a flowerbed, it was the first to use whipstock technology to drill at an angle—three degrees off center, to be precise. The shaft for the well bottomed out 6,618 feet directly beneath the capitol. In one of the richest oil fields in the world, Petunia was one of its star producers. In its first month of service, it produced 14,747 barrels of oil. By August 1942, it was producing a daily average of 831 barrels. By the time the well was capped in 1986, it had produced over 1.5 million barrels of oil during its 44-year lifespan. The state earned 25 percent royalties for all wells on its property.

On November 19, 1945, Gov. Robert S. Kerr opened the third National Aviation Clinic in the House of Representatives chamber at the capitol. President Truman had indicated he would attend the opening ceremony for the clinic but had to cancel a few days before the conference. The clinic brought attendees from across the globe to Oklahoma City and resulted in a resolution calling for the unification of the armed forces.

This view looking east was taken from the gallery of the Senate chamber. Photographs of Gov. Roy Turner and Pres. Harry Truman flank the presiding officer's seat on the rostrum, indicating the image was captured between 1947 and 1951. A sign in the east gallery indicates the section was segregated for black visitors.

PRESS TABLE

The floor of the Senate chamber was the site of one of the most bizarre episodes in the history of the capitol on May 7, 1947. Around 2:00 p.m., Rep. Jimie Scott from Hughes County came over to the chamber. He spoke briefly to Sen. Tom Anglin and then drew his pistol and shot the senator in the left hip. Anglin staggered back and then drew his own pistol to return fire. Accounts differ as to whether Anglin fired his weapon, but he said later he did not. This image is a graphic from the *Daily Oklahoman* describing where the parties were located when the shooting occurred. Anglin was taken to the hospital where he later recovered. Scott was mum about the motive for the shooting, but speculation centered on the fact that Anglin's law firm was representing his wife in divorce proceedings. It was not Anglin's first time being involved in gunplay. In 1931, he was charged with assault with intent to kill the editor of the *Holdenville Daily News*. He was later acquitted.

Despite the proliferation of oil wells around the capitol, the landscaping on the grounds adjacent to the building had undergone much improvement by the time this photograph was taken in 1947. Bermuda and ryegrass were planted in 1936. In 1939, grounds staff obtained trees, shrubs, and flowers from the nursery at Oklahoma A&M, which were planted around the capitol and other state buildings.

In this January 1948 image, capitol superintendent Chet Smith analyzes damage to one of the marble columns in the supreme court chamber due to a fire in a basement storage room. Two months after this photograph was taken, Smith reported to the Joint Appropriations Committee that the capitol was a "fire hazard" and noted four of the five boilers were "in very bad condition."

Even after the completion of the new National Guard Armory and state office building in 1938, office space was still in short supply in the capitol. This photograph shows employees of the board of affairs working in a third floor (originally mezzanine) corridor. The corridor showcases an original plaster barrel-vaulted ceiling, marble floor, and original hollow steel doors.

The capitol looks serene blanketed in snow in this January 1949 photograph. According to the January 26 edition of the *Daily Oklahoman*, a heavy winter system blew into Oklahoma and "set new records for the amount of harsh weather thrown at the state." Wind gusts up to 30 miles per hour resulted in snowdrifts all over Oklahoma City.

By the late 1940s, Governor Marland's action to open up drilling on state property in the 1930s resulted in every available site in the median of Lincoln Boulevard being snatched up. By 1942, 24 wells had been drilled on the state-owned property around the capitol. It is no wonder longtime tour guide Henry Wade's 1975 book on the capitol was titled *Ship of State on a Sea of Oil.*

Capitol workers Mack Collins (left) and Harold Parker Jr. install acoustic ceiling tiles in the Senate chamber in this 1949 photograph. As sound systems became more prevalent, there was a desire to enhance sound quality and reduce echoes in various rooms of the capitol. Over the next couple of decades, acoustic tiles would be adhered to original plaster ceilings, and drop-in ceilings would be installed without regard for historic preservation.

Five

THE CHANGING CHAMBERS

1951–1970

In 1952, the Hugh S. May Company was paid $12,000 for renovation work in the House of Representatives area of the capitol. The scaffolding in this photograph was erected in the House chamber to repaint the ceiling. The members' lounge, anterooms, and restrooms adjacent to the chamber also received a new coat of paint. The renovation also included a sound system and new member desks.

This 1953 image looks south along Lincoln Boulevard to the north entrance of the capitol. A beehive of commercial activity had grown up around NE Twenty-Third Street and Lincoln Boulevard to cater to travelers along Route 66. The Oklahoma State Capitol is one of two capitols in the United States on Route 66. The Illinois Capitol is the other.

In 1953, Lt. Gov. James E. Berry resurrected the idea of constructing a $3.5 million tower on the capitol due to limited office space in the building. The rendering in this photograph was prepared by the Oklahoma City architecture firm of Hudgins, Thompson, Ball, and Associates. Berry's idea gained some traction when Sen. Fred Chapman passed a bill out of the Senate, but the House never took up the measure.

In 1953, Senate Bill 368 was signed into law creating the Capitol Improvement and Zoning District. The law required the production of a master plan for the development of the area around the capitol, which was completed in 1954. The master plan addressed critical issues such as traffic flow around the capitol, parking, recommendations for the placement of additional public buildings, and landscaping.

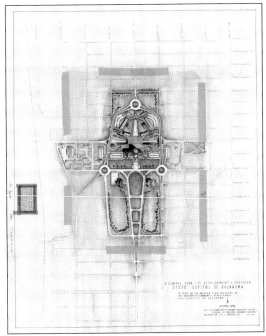

The *Daily Oklahoman* called January 10, 1955, a "cold, biting day." Members of the committee overseeing the inauguration of Raymond Gary arrived at the capitol at 4:30 a.m. to start removing snow from the seats and stands prior to the 11:00 a.m. start time. The newspaper reported the "site of the inauguration was slicked up and dry before the crowd began to gather." Despite the weather, 5,000 people attended the ceremony.

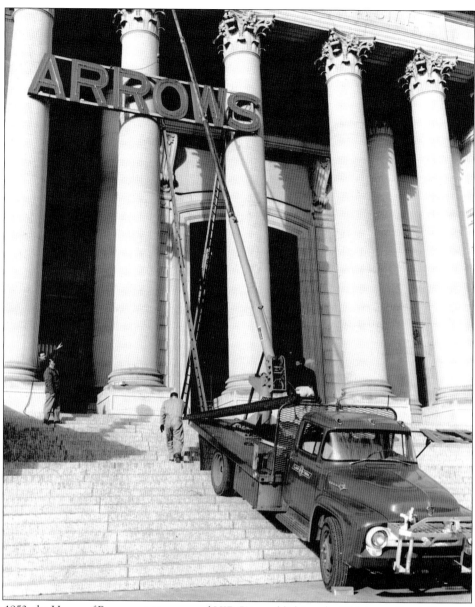

In 1953, the House of Representatives passed HJR 511 establishing the Oklahoma Semi-Centennial Commission. The commission's role was to celebrate Oklahoma's 50th anniversary of statehood in 1957 by planning rodeos, festivals, parades, American Indian dances, and other activities. The semi-centennial year was kicked off on January 9, 1957, at the capitol with a special evening "jubi-light" ceremony hosted by Gov. Raymond Gary. In this photograph, workers are erecting signage on the front of the capitol for the ceremony depicting the semi-centennial slogan, "Arrows to Atoms." During the event, a bonfire of Christmas trees in the capitol's sunken garden was to be lit by a flaming arrow shot by a member of the Otoe tribe. When the arrow did not light the pile as expected, Governor Gary half-jokingly remarked the board of affairs may have sabotaged the bonfire due to their opposition to having it so close to the oil wells. After the ceremony, Governor Gary's address in the joint legislative session was televised in its entirety for the first time in history by WKY-TV.

The Senate chamber was packed on February 11, 1959, for the vote on the resolution to repeal the prohibition of alcohol in Oklahoma. Prioritized by Gov. J. Howard Edmondson, the measure passed by a vote of 31-13. Oklahoma became the last state to repeal prohibition by a vote of the people on April 7, 1959. During the debate, Sen. Ray Fine said the resolution was "the very image of the devil itself."

Adequate parking had become a significant issue by the time this photograph was taken of legislator vehicles parked on the north lawn of the capitol grounds in 1959. A parking study conducted by the department of highways in 1961 recognized the "critical inadequacy of the present parking facilities in the State Capitol Area" and recommended underground parking be constructed in the southwest and northwest lawn directly adjacent to the building.

Overcrowding in the capitol forced the pardon and parole board into the east corridor of the first floor when the legislative session started in 1960. Gov. Johnston Murray contemplated building a new office building in 1953 for $2.5 million, but the proposal stalled. In March 1960, the Oklahoma Capitol Improvement Authority authorized $10 million for the construction of new office buildings in the capitol complex.

A bitter standoff between the Senate and Gov. J. Howard Edmondson resulted in the 28th session being called the "longest in the history of the state" by the *Daily Oklahoman* on July 30, 1961. In this photograph, representatives relax at their desks in the House chamber while waiting for the last few bills to make their way through the process. The House adjourned at 10:53 p.m. on July 29.

In 1961, the board of affairs initiated a restoration project for the capitol, state office building, and the historical society building. A wet aggregate sand-blasting procedure was used on the Indiana limestone and a dry mixture was used on the Tishomingo red granite. The windows on the building were repainted, new mortar was installed in the stone joints, damaged stones were repaired, door and window joints were caulked, and a silicone sealer was applied to the limestone. Accepted remedies at the time such as sandblasting the limestone and the application of the sealer would later be viewed as having a negative effect on the building by restoration experts due to interference with the limestone's natural process for expelling excess moisture. The project concluded in 1962.

CAPITOL BUILDING DURING STRUCTURAL RESTORATION

University of Oklahoma landscape architect Robert Rucker oversaw the design for improving the grounds around the capitol in 1962. The plan called for removing all trees and shrubs and replacing them with 54 varieties of trees native to Oklahoma. The board of affairs, capitol improvement authority, and capitol zoning commission approved a budget of $100,000 for the work.

One aspect of the 1962 beautification plan provided for the installation of 76 new 1,000-watt mercury vapor lights. The Lamar Company in Shawnee installed the floodlights, which provided a blue-white illumination to the building. The company also installed spotlights to highlight some of the featured landscaping. A total of $33,370 was spent on the lighting upgrades.

The state capitol complex changed drastically with the addition of two new state office buildings north of the capitol in 1962 (foreground). This 1968 aerial photograph shows the new Sequoyah Building (left) and Will Rogers Building. One building was originally planned, but a structure large enough to accommodate the state's additional office space requirements would have towered over the capitol.

Jenny Reeser, a member of the Kiltie Band, performed at the capitol on September 1, 1962, as part of a two-day festival to celebrate the completion of the Will Rogers and Sequoyah office buildings. Guests were given guided tours of the capitol and the new office buildings. Governor Edmondson and speaker J.D. McCarty participated in a tree-planting ceremony. A fireworks show capped off the celebration.

The unexpected death of US senator Robert S. Kerr on January 1, 1963, shocked Oklahomans. He was one of the state's most successful oil company entrepreneurs. Elected governor in 1942, he deftly navigated the state through World War II. He was known as the "Uncrowned King of the Senate" at the time of his death. He lay in state in the second-floor rotunda of the capitol on January 3, 1963.

When Senator Kerr died, Governor Edmondson was at the Orange Bowl football game in Miami, Florida. Consequently, Lt. Gov. George Nigh was the acting governor with the power to appoint a new US senator. Nigh declined to do so but ultimately agreed to appoint Governor Edmondson to the post a few days later upon his resignation. Nigh served as governor for nine days before Henry Bellmon was inaugurated.

Prior to the start of the 29th legislature in January 1963, the Senate chamber was outfitted with a public address system for the first time. In this photograph, Louie R. Geiser, secretary of the Senate, inspects one of the desk microphones on the chamber floor to ensure it is in proper working order.

To coincide with the August 28, 1963, March on Washington for Jobs and Freedom, the Oklahoma City chapter of the Congress of Racial Equality marched from the Avery AME chapel to the capitol in a mock funeral procession declaring their intent to "bury" segregation. Some of the signs posted near the casket decry "token" integration, job discrimination, and segregated amusement parks. About 200 people participated in the march.

The Blue Room, originally labeled the stateroom on the capitol's architectural drawings, had seen numerous changes over the years. It had been partitioned as office space for the Department of Public Welfare during the administration of Gov. William H. Murray. Governor Marland redecorated the room with items from his own collection in the late 1930s. By the 1960s, it was regularly used as a conference room. Gov. Henry Bellmon characterized the room as a "shoddy mess" when he asked the legislature to appropriate $55,000 to renovate it in 1963. This 1966 rendering captures the classic look that Governor Bellmon hoped to achieve when the project was completed later that year. Explaining his vision, designer Warren Ramsey said, "We like to visualize the redecoration as historical design that might have been present with the early people." The walls in the room were painted blue and the ceiling was finished in beige with gold accents. Sitting areas were created with new furniture. The focal piece was a $9,000 breakfront that had once resided in a castle in Scotland.

In 1965, one of the biggest scandals in the history of the Oklahoma state government erupted when three members of the Oklahoma Supreme Court were accused of taking bribes to sway their opinions in cases before the court. In 1964, while serving a sentence in federal prison for tax evasion, former supreme court justice N.S. Corn gave an affidavit admitting to accepting bribes and implicating Justices Earl Welch and N.B. Johnson in the practice. The 73-year-old Welch denied guilt but chose to resign. Johnson did not resign, and in March 1965, the House of Representatives overwhelmingly voted to advance two articles of impeachment to the Senate. The Senate organized the court of impeachment in April and the trial began in May. In this photograph, Justice Johnson speaks to reporters outside the Senate chamber after being removed from office on May 12, 1965. The scandal resulted in systematic changes in the way appellate judges were selected to insulate them from political pressure.

In 1963, Charles Banks Wilson, from Miami, Oklahoma, was commissioned to paint four portraits of influential Oklahomans to be placed in the fourth-floor rotunda. The portrait of Will Rogers was the first to be completed in 1964. Linda Dawson (left) and Sandra Dine admire the life-size portrait of Rogers standing on a grass airstrip during their visit to the capitol in 1966.

In 1966, a terrazzo version of the Great Seal of the State of Oklahoma was installed in the first-floor rotunda of the capitol. The seal's design was based on a painting that was produced by Paul LeFebvre for *Oklahoma Today* magazine. The Oklahoma Great Seal was adopted during the constitutional convention based on the design proposed for the State of Sequoyah in 1905.

Lt. Col. Erman Winner of the National Guard's 45th Infantry Division said the 1967 inauguration ceremony of Gov. Dewey Bartlett had more military presence than any of the previous four he had been involved in. Following Bartlett's swearing-in, four artillery guns situated on the west side of the capitol grounds fired a 19-gun salute. The artillery caused several small grass fires, which had to be extinguished after the salute.

This January 1967 photograph shows the dismantling of one of the oil derricks south of the capitol. The derricks were no longer needed due to the availability of modern well servicing equipment. In 1968, a resolution was introduced in the House of Representatives calling for the state to acquire one or more of the derricks to remain on display as historical monuments.

Gen. George M. Johnson brought along some firepower for the first meeting of Gov. Dewey Bartlett's Air Education Committee on July 31, 1968. This AGM-28 Hound Dog cruise missile was parked north of the capitol along NE Twenty-Third Street. The missile was carried under the wing of a B-52 bomber and was armed with a nuclear warhead.

When the Blue Room was renovated in 1966, the former ladies' lounge on the second floor was converted to a conference room and media area for the governor. This 1969 photograph shows the suspended acoustical ceiling installed during the renovation. Rods for television lights were added on the walls, and a rug was laid on the marble floor.

The House of Representatives chamber underwent its biggest modification to date when an enclosure was constructed in the east gallery in the late 1960s. This photograph, dated March 4, 1969, shows a legislator addressing a group of schoolchildren. In later years, the enclosure would be modified to add an area for members of the press.

The Senate continued to modernize its legislative chamber as the decade drew to a close. In the summer of 1969, Ronald Walker, with the International Roll Call Corporation, demonstrated a new electronic voting system in the Senate members' lounge that would be utilized when the second session of the 32nd legislature began in January 1970. It was estimated the new system would save a month's worth of time each session.

During the 1970 legislative interim, the Senate initiated a remodeling project that significantly altered the original design of its chamber. Ornamental plaster scrollwork was removed from the walls and wood paneling replaced it. A new glassed-in press box was installed in the east visitor gallery. Oklahoma City contractor Walter Neshert characterized the renovation as a "desecration" and remarked, "sad indeed is the passing of beauty."

Frank Brown, a painting contractor from Tecumseh, won the bid to repaint the cloud scene on the ceiling of the capitol's saucer dome. The workers on the 68-foot scaffolding in this September 1970 photograph are Patrick Bolin of Oklahoma City (white shirt at top), Joe Trolinger of Tecumseh (dark shirt just below Bolin), and Ronald Walden of Tecumseh.

Six

PROTEST, CELEBRATION, AND MOURNING

1971–1990

When the 33rd legislature convened on January 5, 1971, senators met in a chamber that had been remodeled the previous year. Ornamental plaster framing nooks had been demolished in favor of new wood paneling. The House of Representatives had also undertaken a renovation project, although the results were not as drastic. The House chamber received a lighting upgrade and new paint.

The onset of the 1970s was a time of great change on the state capitol campus. As early as the 1940s, the board of affairs had considered major changes to the street infrastructure around the capitol to address traffic and parking problems. A master plan in 1960 called for Lincoln Boulevard to be rerouted around the building, but it drew opposition from Lincoln Terrace residents. After another master planning effort in 1966, work was finally ready to begin in 1971. On land that was previously occupied by oil wells south of the capitol, a new parking lot was created (above). Officials moved ahead with diverting Lincoln Boulevard, and a freeway-style cloverleaf system was created to facilitate traffic flow. To connect the capitol campus, NE Twenty-Third Street was converted to an underpass (below).

The capitol rotunda became a movie set on August 3, 1972, for the filming of *Thirty Dangerous Seconds*. First-time stuntman Robert Stone was paid $150 to hurl himself over the railing in the fourth-floor rotunda with a crowd of 150 spectators watching. Stone rigged a canvas net on the second floor to catch his fall. Much to his relief, he successfully completed the stunt in one take.

Ed Keens, chief porter for the Oklahoma Senate, carts the silver punch bowl from the USS *Oklahoma* to the Senate members' lounge for a reception on the opening day of session in 1973. In 1913, the legislature appropriated $7,500 for the creation of the 55-piece silver set to reside on the new battleship. The silver service was removed just prior to the Japanese attack on Pearl Harbor in 1941.

This photograph from May 1973 provides a unique view of the monumental south portico of the capitol. Ten massive Corinthian columns greet visitors who just walked up 26 granite steps to reach the portico. The July 1, 1917, *Daily Oklahoman* characterized the front entrance to the capitol as "a triumph of beauty and architectural skill."

In June 1974, a chunk of plaster from the capitol ceiling came loose and fell in the fourth-floor rotunda. The rotunda was subsequently closed until the ceiling could be inspected and repairs made. In this photograph, workers from Cunningham Plastering Company of Oklahoma City erect scaffolding to reach the high ceiling. The company was given a $12,000 contract for the work.

This 1974 photograph looks south toward the capitol from the median of Lincoln Boulevard. In a 2001 interview with Arnold Hamilton, veteran capitol journalist Frosty Troy recalled the days when the motels and restaurants north of the capitol were "teeming with lawmakers and lobbyists." Unfortunately, as the 1980s approached, the commercial area north of the capitol went into a slow but steady decline.

By 1975, the capitol complex had grown significantly. New state office buildings had been constructed north of the Sequoyah and Will Rogers buildings. Completed in 1974, the Oliver Hodge and M.C. Connors buildings housed the department of education and tax commission, respectively. Also completed in 1974 was a building for the Allen Wright Memorial Library (far upper right). The department of transportation building was added in 1975 (upper right).

In 1970, renowned artist Charles Banks Wilson was called upon once again to beautify the fourth-floor rotunda of the capitol. He was commissioned by the legislature to create four large murals that would chronicle Oklahoma's history from the entrance of the Spanish explorers in 1541 to white settlement in the late 1800s. Prior to beginning work on the 13-by-26-foot canvases, Wilson sculpted plasteline clay models commenting, "This was common practice by masters of the Renaissance, modeling a composition in clay. It isn't done much today." The murals took four years to complete and were entitled *Discovery and Exploration*, *Frontier Trade*, *Indian Immigration*, and *Non-Indian Settlement*. They were painted using polymer acrylic paint and each canvas was mounted on fiberglass supports before being hoisted into place by Wynn Construction Company of Oklahoma City. The legislature paid Wilson $65,000 for his work. At the dedication ceremony on Statehood Day in 1976, University of Oklahoma historian Dr. A.M. Gibson remarked, "He has struck a true epic in each of these murals."

Sunday, July 4, 1976, marked 200 years since the signing of the Declaration of Independence. To commemorate the nation's bicentennial, a day-long celebration took place on the capitol grounds and inside the building with musical performances representing various cultures. In this photograph, Gov. David Boren participates in a morning flag-raising ceremony prior to the commencement of festivities. Over 10,000 people visited the capitol that day.

In this 1977 photograph, popular capitol tour guide Henry F. "Hank" Wade poses outside the front entrance of the capitol. Wade lost both of his hands in a work-related electrical accident in 1937. He began giving tours at the capitol in 1962. With the assistance of the Oklahoma Historical Society, he published a book about the capitol, *Ship of State on a Sea of Oil*, in 1975.

Oklahoma City architectural firm Meyer-Brown designed new House of Representatives and Senate committee rooms to infill the fourth-floor corridors flanking the grand staircase in the south wing of the capitol. The rooms utilized glass walls to keep the original architectural details of the corridors visible. Shown in this 1977 photograph, the completed renovation won awards from the American Institute of Steel Construction and the American Institute of Architects.

On February 28, 1978, over 100 Langston University students staged an overnight sit-in in the House of Representatives chamber and lobby to protest a lack of funding for the school. Lawrence Cudjoe, basketball coach at Langston, commented, "The whites have universities scattered all over the state. Our people have only got that one little step-child out there and they're trying to kill it." The protest ended peacefully the next day.

On May 26, 1978, three Oklahoma Highway Patrol troopers, Houston F. "Pappy" Summers, Billy G. Young, and Pat Grimes, were killed in a shoot-out with prison escapees in Bryan County. Two days later, the three troopers laid in state in the first-floor rotunda of the capitol. Hundreds of people filed by the caskets to pay their respects. Highway patrol officers came from around the country to honor their fallen comrades.

Gov. David Boren's 1977 proposal to use federal funds to beautify the grounds south of the capitol by adding a small lake where the parking lot had recently been installed was deridingly called "Lake Boren" by some legislators. The proposal never really took off due to estimates that came in higher than available funds. However, some improvements were made, including new sidewalks, as shown in this June 1978 image.

Below-zero temperatures and a blanket of snow greeted workers responsible for completing preparations for the inauguration of George Nigh as Oklahoma's 22nd governor on January 8, 1979. As the ceremony began, the temperature had inched up to 15 degrees. Upon observing that some people had left to seek warmth, the new governor remarked, "The world is run by those who stay until the end of the meeting."

Senate chief sergeant-at-arms Bob Craig works at his desk in the Senate chamber in January 1980, preparing for the upcoming opening day of the legislative session. Before coming to the Senate, Craig played on the University of Oklahoma's 1968 Orange Bowl championship football team. Upon his retirement after 50 years of service in 2020, Senate Resolution 13 praised his "enduring legacy of service and loyalty."

Local artists display their creations in this January 16, 1980, art show in the fourth-floor rotunda of the capitol. The show was sponsored by the Oklahoma Arts Council to provide an opportunity for legislators to choose artwork for their offices. The Oklahoma Arts Council was formed in 1965 to allow the state to access federal funding for arts education and creation. The agency also manages the Capitol Art Collection.

California artist Robert Yoakum created this 11-foot wooden eagle with a gold overlay to honor the Americans held hostage in Iran. The eagle toured the United States and was placed in the capitol's first-floor rotunda during its temporary residency in Oklahoma. This January 15, 1981, photograph was taken five days before the 52 hostages were released.

On March 16, 1982, Ronald Reagan became the only sitting president of the United States to visit the Oklahoma State Capitol (left). The president was in Oklahoma to promote his "new federalism" agenda. Reagan opened his speech in the House of Representatives chamber in front of a joint session of the legislature by saying, "No other state exemplifies the American experience than does Oklahoma." He also acknowledged Oklahoma's 75th anniversary by joking, "I don't get too many chances to be around someone or something older than I am." Security measures were tight at the capitol for the president's visit. His limousine was driven into the building at the west entrance, and metal detectors were placed at the entrances to the House chamber. While the president was speaking, protestors were allowed to congregate in designated areas on the south side of the capitol (below).

Fourteen-year-old Anna Long (left), an eighth-grader at Casady School in Oklahoma City, and 17-year-old Penny King (right), a junior at Putnam City High School, prepare to leave the capitol after serving as pages in the House of Representatives in May 1982. The House and Senate page program gives students the opportunity to learn about the legislative process while performing duties for the members of each body.

On March 31, 1982, members of Bacone College's Indian Club performed traditional dances in the first-floor rotunda of the capitol. The event was associated with the Oklahoma Indian Youth Art Festival. Founded as The Indian University in 1880, the Muskogee, Oklahoma, institution seeks to produce "transformational leaders in both Native and non-native communities."

Richard Thorpe, son of legendary Oklahoma-born athlete Jim Thorpe, stands in front of his father's capitol rotunda portrait by Charles Banks Wilson in 1983. To portray Jim Thorpe's athletic features, Wilson used multiple athletes as models and even the forearm of a bricklayer and the deltoid of a farm laborer. Wilson characterized Thorpe as "the nearest thing to a Greek god."

Visitors to the capitol during the holiday season in 1985 were greeted with a new sight: a 25-foot-tall poinsettia Christmas tree. The new display was controversial at first due to the cost of a $10,000 metal stand to hold the flowers. A real tree would once again reign in the first-floor rotunda in 1990 until the poinsettia tree returned in 1993. The poinsettia tree was retired for good in 1999.

Phillips Petroleum Company formally donated State Capitol Well No. 1 to the Oklahoma Historical Society in a ceremony on August 18, 1986. At left is Phillips official Robert Wallace and at right is the director of the Oklahoma Historical Society, Denzil Garrison. Also known as "Petunia No. 1," the well was plugged in 1986 after producing over $1 million in royalties and gross production taxes for the state.

Vietnam War veteran Mike Mullings stands in front of the Oklahoma Veterans Memorial on the grounds of the Oklahoma Historical Society building on November 11, 1986, the day it was dedicated. Jay O'Meilia and Bill Sowell sculpted the eight-foot-tall bronze statue of a weary soldier coming off a patrol in Vietnam. Unfinished when it was dedicated, Mullings continued to raise funds for the memorial until it was completed in 1994.

When Gov. Henry Bellmon wanted his title painted above the door to his office, Gary Hoppis, construction foreman for the department of human services, was ready to perform the task. This photograph from the January 16, 1988, *Daily Oklahoman* shows Hoppis discovering the desired lettering was already lurking beneath a sheet of wood paneling.

On May 13, 1988, a riot broke out after a fight between inmates over stolen property at the Mack Alford Correctional Center, a medium-security facility near Stringtown. Eight prison guards were taken hostage and over $7 million in damage was sustained after two housing units were burned. On May 25, the eight guards and two hostage negotiators were honored with a resolution in the House of Representatives.

Once covered over and converted to office space, this beautiful marble staircase connecting the first and second floors of the capitol was completely restored and officially reopened during a special ceremony on April 22, 1989. Helen Arnold (left), director of the office of public affairs, and Don Price, building manager, review the completed work prior to the opening.

By 1989, the Oklahoma State Capitol had eclipsed 70 years of service to the state. The building had seen many changes over the years, from the proliferation of oil derricks on the grounds to significant interior renovations. The one thing the capitol did not have yet was its long-awaited dome. As recently as 1988, legislators had suggested a task force to study the idea, but to no avail.

Comanche medicine man George Woogee Watchetaker holds a clay pot of blessed water that he used to pour on the feet of the new 14-foot-tall bronze statue *As Long as the Waters Flow* by Allan Houser on June 4, 1989. The statue was commissioned by the Oklahoma Arts Council and depicts a woman of the red earth with an eagle feather fan. Houser is standing to the left of Watchetaker.

A group of teachers from Stillwater gather on the south plaza on Monday, April 16, 1990, to rally for the passage of HB 1017, a monumental education reform bill. Approximately 10,000 teachers walked off the job and came to the capitol for a week of protests. The bill, which appropriated new money for education and limited classroom sizes, was later passed and signed by Governor Bellmon on April 24.

Seven

THE LONG-AWAITED DOME

1991–2002

David Walters, the 39-year-old owner of a commercial real estate company, was inaugurated as Oklahoma's 24th governor on January 14, 1991, in front of a crowd of approximately 5,000 people. In his speech, Walters, from the western Oklahoma town of Canute, said, "I promise you today that this is one farm boy who's not going to forget his roots."

Prior to being sworn in as governor, David Walters considered making the ornate, two-story-tall Blue Room his office. Critics of the plan noted the Blue Room was twice as large as the Oval Office in the White House and any changes to the room would need to be approved by the Capitol Preservation Commission. He later backed off the proposal and the room continued in its ceremonial capacity.

Operation Desert Storm, also known as the Gulf War, began on January 17, 1991, and concluded on February 28, 1991. A rally was held on the steps of the capitol on March 17 to welcome troops from the Airborne Warning and Control Wing stationed at Tinker Air Force Base back to Oklahoma. More than 1,000 people came out to show their support for the returning soldiers.

In 1988, the legislature authorized the creation of the Indian Flag Plaza and appropriated $99,000 to get the project started. Construction on the plaza, located north of the NE Twenty-Third Street underpass between the Will Rogers and Sequoyah buildings, began in 1991. The plaza was designed in homage to the ancient Spiro Mounds and would feature the flags of 38 tribal governments. Funding issues delayed its completion until 1995.

When the capitol was completed in 1917, the building's interior lacked color due to insufficient funding. In 1991, a $60,000 appropriation from the legislature allowed the fourth and fifth floors of the building to be painted. New base colors called roasted almond and imported ivory were accented by Mozart melon, gold leaf, opal basil, and powder blue. In this photograph, painters work above the grand staircase on lifts and scaffolding.

In 1988, Sen. Jerry Smith worked with the director of the Oklahoma Arts Council, Betty Price, to commission a mural honoring the Five Moons, the American Indian prima ballerinas with Oklahoma roots who achieved world renown for their skill and grace beginning in the 1940s. Mike Larsen, an Oklahoma City artist and Chickasaw, was chosen to create the 20-foot-long mural. The ballerinas were portrayed wearing white dresses. Scenes in the background of the painting depict the forced removal of American Indians on the Trail of Tears. The ballerinas, characterized as "transformative artists" in a 2021 *New York Times* article, appeared for the first time together at the November 17, 1991, ceremony in the capitol to dedicate the mural. From left to right are Yvonne Chouteau Terekhov, Cherokee; Mike Larsen; Rosella Hightower, Choctaw; Maria Tallchief, Osage; Marjorie Tallchief Skibine, Osage; and Moscelyne Larkin, Shawnee-Peoria.

In 1991, architecture students from the University of Oklahoma built a model of the capitol to show how it would look crowned with the long-hoped-for dome. At right, Carol Guinn, leader of the DOMERS (Dedicated Oklahomans Marshaling Excellence and Rallying Spirit), smiles as Lou Kerr, chair of the Capitol Preservation Commission, and Raymond Yeh, dean of the University of Oklahoma College of Architecture, look on.

During the weekend of December 28–29, 1991, the state capitol and surrounding grounds were closed to visitors by the Federal Aviation Administration so helicopters could remove old air conditioning equipment from the roof of the building. The $4.7 million project was overseen by R&M Mechanical Contractors from Norman. It took approximately 70 airlifts to remove the old equipment and place the new units.

After an infestation of roaches closed the cafeteria in the basement of the capitol in mid-1991, the legislature appropriated $40,000 to refurbish the eatery. The newly dubbed Red Earth Café featured a decorative motif described as a cross between New Orleans and Red Earth. Chef Charles Duit (left) was responsible for food preparation while the café was managed by Jim Sellers (right). It opened on February 8, 1992.

Schoolchildren packed the Blue Room on March 4, 1993, to hear Governor Walters and his wife, Rhonda, announce a series of initiatives created to help children in the state. The proposals were estimated to cost $11.5 million and included plans to reduce child abuse, provide additional health and social services, and expand access to prenatal care.

Men's fancy dance champion Amos Littlecrow waits to exhibit his skills in the fourth-floor capitol rotunda beneath the watchful gaze of Will Rogers in Charles Banks Wilson's famous portrait. The March 12, 1993, exhibition by American Indian performers served as a preview for the upcoming Red Earth Festival in Oklahoma City.

An article in the June 4, 1993, *Daily Oklahoman* lamented the downfall of North Lincoln Boulevard, the main corridor from Interstate 44 to the capitol. Abandoned motels, shuttered businesses, tall weeds, and trash had come to characterize the thoroughfare. In the late 1990s, Gov. Frank Keating instituted the Lincoln Renaissance program for the state to acquire dilapidated properties, install new landscaping, and clean up the approach.

As part of a sister state exchange program, a group of Japanese high school students and their chaperones from Kyoto, Japan, visited the state capitol in July 1993. The agricultural exchange program was overseen by Lt. Gov. Jack Mildren. In this photograph, Kaiko Tsujisato directs the visitors to line up for a photograph on the south steps of the capitol.

For the first time since 1990, the poinsettia Christmas tree returned to the capitol in December 1993. Approximately 600 poinsettia flowers were placed on the metal stand that reached 25 feet tall. Nancy Denton with the Department of Tourism said, "I hope everybody will come out and see it because it is kind of a Christmas present for the public and the citizens of the state—something they can really be proud of."

In July 1993, with $1 million in bond funding at its disposal, the Senate undertook a chamber restoration project to make amends for the 1970 remodeling work that removed the historic architectural flourishes from the room. As overseen by capitol architect Paul Meyer, the project aimed to return the chamber to its 1917 roots. Clerestory windows that had been covered in favor of air conditioning ductwork were revealed and the drop-in ceiling was removed. Original ornamental plaster detailing was restored and new stained-glass skylights were created to match what had been there before. The wood paneling that lined the walls was removed and new plaster picture niches were fashioned. Included in the project was the removal of the glassed-in press gallery from the east side of the chamber and its relocation to the west side of the gallery. In this photograph, taken in December 1993 when the project was near completion, Michael McMillan applies a faux marble paint finish to a railing in the visitor gallery of the chamber.

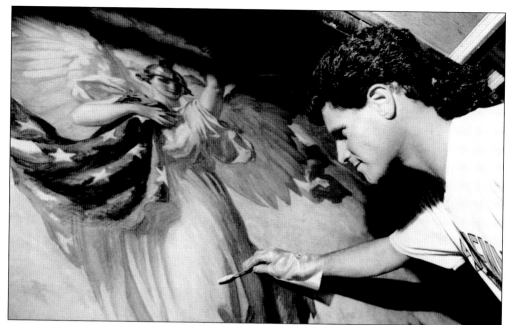

In October 1994, the triptych painting *Pro Patria* was professionally cleaned for the first time since it was installed in 1928. Carmen Bria with the nationally renowned Western Center for the Conservation of Fine Arts goes about the delicate work with a cotton swab from scaffolding high above the grand staircase. The project cost $14,000 and included cleaning the glass on the committee room enclosures flanking the staircase.

In 1982, bronze busts of 21 Oklahoma governors were commissioned as part of the Diamond Jubilee Commission's mission to celebrate the 75th anniversary of statehood. The busts were sculpted by Leonard McMurry and placed in the second-floor rotunda of the capitol. In November 1994, the second-floor southwest monumental corridor was restored and the busts were relocated there. The corridor was renamed the Hall of Governors.

Gov. Frank Keating speaks to the press in February 1995. Describing the capitol during the 1970s as "gray and dark," he made a priority of beautifying the building and its grounds during his two terms in office. In a July 2000 speech, he said, "A statement of our poverty is the absence of a dome; the statement of our prosperity is a dome and completion of this building."

The 14 Flags Plaza at the south entrance of the capitol was dedicated by Governor Bellmon in 1966. The display exhibited flags that flew over Oklahoma from 1541 to 1925. In 1987, Rep. Don Ross called on the governor to remove the Confederate flag. It was not returned after a 1988 renovation of the plaza despite an order by the legislature, hence the empty flagpole seen here in 1995.

In the 1980s, Sen. John Dahl started the annual tradition of honoring the impact of legendary western swing bandleader Bob Wills by sponsoring Bob Wills Day at the capitol every spring. Bob Wills cemented his legacy in Oklahoma music history by moving his innovative band, the Playboys, to Tulsa from Waco, Texas, in 1934. Now performing under the moniker Bob Wills and his Texas Playboys, they performed regular shows during the noon hour on radio station KVOO. From 1935 to 1942, they broadcast from Cain's Dancing Academy. With their music amplified by KVOO's strong signal, they became one of the most popular bands in the country. In 1988, the legislature designated Wills's song "Faded Love" as Oklahoma's official country and western song. During Bob Wills Day at the capitol festivities, fiddle players and bands from all over the state would perform for legislators in the House and Senate chambers and the rotunda for visitors and staff. In this photograph, Bob Saylor plays his fiddle in the fourth-floor rotunda on April 10, 1995.

At 9:02 a.m. on April 19, 1995, an ammonium nitrate-fuel oil bomb housed in a Ryder truck exploded in front of the Alfred P. Murrah Federal Building in downtown Oklahoma City. The blast killed 168 people and damaged more than 300 buildings in the vicinity. Timothy McVeigh and Terry Nichols were arrested and convicted for the crime that was deemed the worst domestic terrorist act in US history up to that point. A few days after the bombing, a memorial service was held at the capitol, which included a ceremonial releasing of balloons from the front steps (above). On May 11, 1995, volunteers and rescue workers crowded into the House chamber where they were honored with a resolution and speeches of appreciation by members of the legislative body.

The lunette mural *We Belong to the Land* is hoisted into place over the entrance to the House of Representatives chamber in early 1999. Jeff Dodd painted the mural as a tribute to Oklahoma's agricultural history. The Oklahoma Centennial Commission chose to commission this mural as its first project to celebrate 100 years of statehood.

The House of Representatives undertook a major restoration of its chamber after the conclusion of the legislative session in 1999. Much like the earlier Senate chamber restoration, a concerted effort was made to return the chamber to its World War I–era look. Discussing the $1.2 million effort, speaker Lloyd Benson said, "This chamber has been lovingly restored to the beauty and splendor originally envisioned by the founders of our state."

With $17 million in private funds pledged and another $5 million authorized in bond financing, the project to construct a dome for the capitol was announced by Governor Keating in July 2000. Capitol Dome Builders, a joint venture between Manhattan Construction and Flintco, was formed to execute the work. FSB was selected as the architectural firm. A dome-raising ceremony was held on June 20, 2001, to officially start the monumental task.

In designing the dome, FSB consulted Layton and Smith's original plans. It was decided that modern construction methods would be used in constructing the dome. Instead of a concrete structural frame, steel would be used. Instead of limestone cladding, precast concrete blocks allowed for uniformity of color and size. The use of these materials reduced the completion time and produced a lighter structure.

An open call was made for artists to submit clay models for the dome's finial sculpture based on the theme of a "nonspecific American Indian male." Twenty-two artists submitted entries in the blind competition. The winner was Enoch Kelly Haney, a full-blood Seminole/Muscogee Indian and sitting state senator. Haney's design featured a young American Indian warrior, his body oriented to the east while his face looks south. His lance pierces his leggings and is planted in the ground as a sign of bravery and courage. The 5,980-pound, 22-foot-tall bronze sculpture was named *The Guardian*. Commenting on the significance of the piece, Haney said, "I think for Native American people, it's a day of arrival. The sculpture of a Native American person is, in fact, the story of Oklahoma." On June 7, 2002, thousands of people flooded the capitol grounds to see the first statue of an American Indian placed at a capitol in the United States. In this photograph, an American Indian honor guard takes its place in front of the massive warrior.

At the conclusion of ceremonial activities on June 7, 2002, Governor Keating signaled to the construction team that he was ready for *The Guardian* to be raised. Unfortunately, the weight of the sculpture had dipped the crane boom lower than expected, which made the cables too long to set the statue on the first try. After lowering the statue and adjusting the cables, it was set in place on the dome.

After *The Guardian* was lowered into place, Flintco employee Jesus Perez was selected to climb up the narrow chute to secure the sculpture into place with eight one-by-four-inch bolts. In this photograph, members of the construction crew pose with the statue after its installation on June 7, 2002.

A new stained-glass skylight was designed by artists Jim Triffo (right) and Pat Wood (left) to reside in the oculus of the interior dome, 190 feet above the capitol's first floor. The new state seal was 6.5 feet in diameter and more accurate than the plaster seal it replaced. The new 23-foot-diameter skylight cost $50,000 and over 9,000 man-hours to construct.

The capitol's stunning interior dome was designed to pay homage to Oklahoma's state wildflower, the gaillardia. The 192 gold rosettes with red backgrounds resemble the petals, while the green color evokes the stem. A blue ring with reddish hues mimics the evening sky at sunset. Upon seeing it for the first time, Tulsa resident Gerry Hayhurst said, "I think it is gorgeous."

On November 12, 2002, Governor Keating (third from left) and Lt. Gov. Mary Fallin (second from right) opened the new Centennial Memorial Plaza of the Oklahomans. The new south plaza was clad in 15,000 granite pavers. It replaced the former concrete surface. Governor Keating remarked, "This project shows how much we value our past and eagerly await our future." The federally funded project cost $3.5 million.

Eighty-five years after construction on the capitol was completed in 1917, the dome was finally installed. On the state's 95th birthday, November 16, 2002, a grand celebration drawing 16,000 people to the capitol grounds commemorated the incredible achievement. Numerous Oklahoma celebrities participated in the ceremony, and a video message from Pres. George W. Bush was played. The evening's festivities culminated in a 25-minute fireworks show.

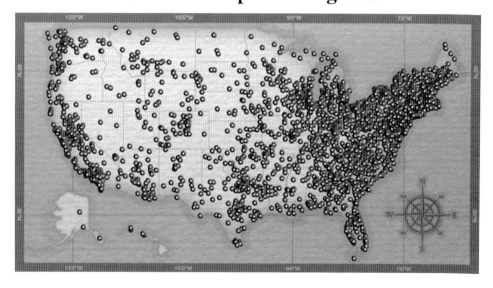